First Facts®

U.S. Military Forces

WITHDRAWN

THE UNITED STATES NAVY

BY MICHAEL GREEN

CAPSTONE PRESS
a capstone imprint

First Facts are published by Capstone Press,
1710 Roe Crest Drive, North Mankato, Minnesota 56003
www.capstonepub.com

Library of Congress Cataloging-in-Publication Data
Green, Michael, 1952–
The United States Navy / by Michael Green.
     p. cm.—(First facts. U.S. Military Forces)
     Summary: "Provides information on the training, missions, and equipment used by the
United States Navy"—Provided by publisher.
     Audience: Grades K-3.
     Includes bibliographical references and index.
     ISBN 978-1-4765-0070-6 (library binding)
     ISBN 978-1-4765-1587-8 (eBook PDF)
1. United States. Navy—Juvenile literature. 2. United States. Navy—History—Juvenile
literature. I. Title.
VA58.4.G74 2013
359.00973—dc23   2012033249

Editorial Credits

Aaron Sautter, editor; Ashlee Suker, designer; Eric Manske, production specialist

Photo Credits

Corbis/Bettmann, 6; U.S. Navy Photo, 21, Lt.j.g. Liza Swart, 13, MC2 Alexander W. Cabrall, 19, MC2 Chelsea
A. Radford, 1, MC2 Eric Tretter, 18, MC2 Joseph M. Buliavac, 9, MC3 Natasha R. Chalk, 10, MCC Eric S.
Powell, 17, MCC Shawn P. Eklund, 15, MCSN John Grandin, cover; U.S. Navy Photo courtesy of General
Dynamics Bath Iron Works, 5

Artistic Effects

Shutterstock: Kirsty Pargeter, Redshinestudio, Vilmos Varga

Printed in the United States of America in North Mankato, Minnesota.
092012   006933CGS13

TABLE OF CONTENTS

CHAPTER ONE

KEEPING THE SEAS SAFE

Near the coast of Somalia, **pirates** begin shooting at a U.S. Navy warship. Navy sailors fire back and destroy the pirates' boat. The pirates jump into the water and are captured. The Navy ship then continues its **mission** to keep the ocean safe.

pirate—a person who attacks and steals from ships at sea

mission—a military task

The U.S. Navy defends the United States and helps keep waterways safe. The Continental Congress created the U.S. Navy on October 13, 1775. It was first known as the Continental navy.

The Navy protects oceans and rivers. But it also fights on land and in the air.

FACT

In January 2010 a huge earthquake hit the country of Haiti. The Navy brought tons of food, fresh water, and supplies to help.

CHAPTER TWO

A POWERFUL NAVAL FORCE

The U.S. Navy is the strongest **naval** force in the world. The Navy has more than 320,000 active sailors. More than 100,000 reserve sailors also serve. Wherever there is a need, the Navy is called to action.

naval—having to do with the navy or warships

Most sailors are **enlisted** men and women. They perform many different jobs. Some are pilots. Others are computer programmers. They work hard to keep ships running smoothly.

Officers lead Navy ships and **bases**. They make decisions and give orders during missions.

FACT

Sailors and officers serve at least one term. Enlisted sailors serve terms that last two to four years. Officers serve for three to five years.

enlist—to voluntarily join a branch of the military

base—an area where people serving in the military live and supplies are stored

CHAPTER THREE

BECOMING A SAILOR

Recruits go to basic training for seven to nine weeks. They do push-ups and sit-ups, swim, and run through **obstacle courses**. Recruits also learn survival skills and how to use weapons.

After boot camp, sailors go to "A" school. They learn skills needed for their Navy jobs. Sailors serve in different jobs, such as lawyers, engineers, and combat specialists.

recruit—a new member of the armed forces

obstacle course—a series of barriers that sailors must jump over, climb, or crawl through

To become Navy officers, sailors attend Officer Candidate School or Officer Development School. There they learn leadership skills needed to **command** a ship or submarine.

College students can join the Naval Reserve Officers Training Corps (NROTC). They take naval skills classes while in school. During summers they learn leadership skills on Navy ships.

command—to have control over something

CHAPTER FOUR

SAILING INTO BATTLE

The U.S. Navy has the world's largest naval **fleet**. It has more than 280 ships and submarines. Aircraft carriers carry thousands of sailors and up to 80 planes.

Cruisers, destroyers, and submarines are mighty warships. They are armed with missiles, **torpedoes**, and powerful machine guns.

fleet—a group of warships under one command

torpedo—an underwater missile

AIRCRAFT CARRIER

EA-18 GROWLER

The Navy also uses more than 3,700 aircraft. Fighter planes are armed with machine guns, missiles, and bombs. E-2C Hawkeyes and EA-18 Growlers use **radar** to find enemy targets.

radar—a device that uses radio waves to track the location of objects

SH-60 Seahawk helicopters strike at enemy targets. The Sea Dragon MH-53E helicopter carries troops and heavy equipment.

SH-60 SEAHAWK

CHAPTER FIVE

DEFENDING FREEDOM

The U.S. Navy uses many powerful weapons. Tomahawk missiles hit targets up to 1,000 miles (1,600 kilometers) away. Aegis Combat Systems can find, track, and destroy up to 100 targets at a time.

The U.S. Navy has the best sailors, ships, and aircraft in the world. It stands strong to defend America and keep the world's waterways safe.

FACT

U.S. Navy Special Forces are called SEALs, which stands for sea, air, and land. They carry out the Navy's most dangerous missions.

GLOSSARY

base (BAYS)—an area where people serving in the military live and supplies are stored

command (kuh-MAND)—to have control over something

enlist (in-LIST)—to voluntarily join a branch of the military

fleet (FLEET)—a group of warships under one command

missile (MISS-uhl)—an explosive weapon that can travel long distances

mission (MISH-uhn)—a military task

naval (NAY-vuhl)—having to do with the navy or warships

obstacle course (OB-stuh-kuhl KORSS)—a series of barriers that sailors must jump over, climb, or crawl through

pirate (PYE-rit)—a person who attacks and steals from ships at sea

radar (RAY-dar)—a device that uses radio waves to track the location of objects

recruit (ri-KROOT)—a new member of the armed forces

torpedo (tor-PEE-doh)—an underwater missile

READ MORE

Besel, Jennifer M. *The Navy SEALs*. Elite Military Forces. Mankato, Minn.: Capstone Press, 2011.

Jackson, Kay. *Navy Ships in Action*. Amazing Military Vehicles. New York: PowerKids Press, 2009.

Nagle, Jeanne. *Navy*. U.S. Military Forces. New York: Gareth Stevens Pub., 2012.

INTERNET SITES

FactHound offers a safe, fun way to find Internet sites related to this book. All of the sites on FactHound have been researched by our staff.

Here's all you do:

Visit *www.facthound.com*

Type in this code: 9781476500706

 Super-cool stuff! Check out projects, games and lots more at **www.capstonekids.com**

INDEX